# Table of Contents

# Homemade Pizza Recipes

# Recipe 1: Chickpea Onion Pizza

Boiled chickpea and white onion toppings pizza!

**Yield:** 6

**Prep Time:** 10 minutes

**Cook Time:** 15 minutes

**Ingredient List:**

- 1 medium pizza base
- 2 cups mozzarella cheese, grated
- 2 cups boiled chickpeas
- 1 large white onion, finely chopped
- 2 tbsp. pizza sauce
- Dried oregano and chilli flakes for seasoning
- Salt and pepper to taste

## Preparation:

1.  Preheat the oven to 350°F.

2.  Spread a pizza sauce over pizza base and sprinkle mozzarella over each half. Add chickpeas and onion to the pizza in an even layer. Add salt and pepper.

3.  Now, place the pizza over oven's grill.

4.  Bake for 15 minutes or until cheese melts down completely and turn golden brown.

5.  Once ready, remove the pizza from oven.

6.  Season with dried oregano and chilli flakes.

7.  Then, transfer the pizza to a serving platter and make 6 equal slices with the help of a pizza cutter

8.  Serve hot!

# Recipe 2:  Red Hot Pepper Pizza

Pizza topped with cayenne pepper, green olives and hot sauce mix!

**Yield:** 6

**Prep Time:** 10 minutes

**Cook Time:** 15 minutes

**Ingredient List:**

- 1 medium pizza base
- 2 cups mozzarella cheese, grated
- 1 cup cayenne pepper, chopped
- 1 cup green olives, chopped
- 1 tsp. hot sauce
- 2 tbsp. pizza sauce
- Dried oregano and chilli flakes for seasoning
- Salt and pepper to taste

нннннннннннннннннннннннннннннннннннннн

**Preparation:**

1. Preheat the oven to 350°F.

2. Combine cayenne pepper, olives and hot sauce in a bowl. Mix well and keep aside.

3. Spread a pizza sauce over pizza base and sprinkle mozzarella over each half. Add prepared mix to the pizza in an even layer. Add salt and pepper.

4. Now, place the pizza over oven's grill.

5. Bake for 15 minutes or until cheese melts down completely and turn golden brown.

6. Once ready, remove the pizza from oven.

7. Season with dried oregano and chilli flakes.

8. Then, transfer the pizza to a serving platter and make 6 equal slices with the help of a pizza cutter

9. Serve hot!

# Recipe 3:  Hawaiian Pizza

Pizza with ham and pineapple!

**Yield:** 6

**Prep Time:** 10 minutes

**Cook Time:** 15 minutes

**Ingredient List:**

- 1 medium pizza base
- 2 cups mozzarella cheese, grated
- 2 cups ham, chopped
- 2 cups pineapple, finely chopped
- 2 tbsp. pizza sauce
- Dried oregano and chilli flakes for seasoning
- Salt and pepper to taste

## Preparation:

1.  Preheat the oven to 350°F.

2.  Spread a pizza sauce over pizza base and sprinkle mozzarella over each half. Add ham and pineapple to the pizza in an even layer. Add salt and pepper.

3.  Now, place the pizza over oven's grill.

4.  Bake for 15 minutes or until cheese melts down completely and turn golden brown.

5.  Once ready, remove the pizza from oven.

6.  Season with dried oregano and chilli flakes.

7.  Then, transfer the pizza to a serving platter and make 6 equal slices with the help of a pizza cutter.

8.  Serve hot!

# Recipe 4: Bacon Pizza

Pizza topped with bacon rashers and mozzarella!

**Yield:** 6

**Prep Time:** 10 minutes

**Cook Time:** 15 minutes

**Ingredient List:**

- 1 medium pizza base
- 2 cups mozzarella cheese, grated
- 2 cups bacon rashers, finely chopped
- 2 tbsp. pizza sauce
- Dried oregano and chilli flakes for seasoning
- Salt and pepper to taste

## Preparation:

1.  Preheat the oven to 350ºF.

2.  Spread a pizza sauce over pizza base and sprinkle mozzarella over each half. Add bacon to the pizza in an even layer. Add salt and pepper.

3.  Now, place the pizza over oven's grill.

4.  Bake for 15 minutes or until cheese melts down completely and turn golden brown.

5.  Once ready, remove the pizza from oven.

6.  Season with dried oregano and chilli flakes.

7.  Then, transfer the pizza to a serving platter and make 6 equal slices with the help of a pizza cutter

8.  Serve hot!

# Recipe 5: Bell Pepper and Onion Pizza

Pizza with green bell pepper and white onion!

**Yield:** 6

**Prep Time:** 10 minutes

**Cook Time:** 15 minutes

**Ingredient List:**

- 1 medium pizza base
- 2 cups mozzarella cheese, grated
- 1 large green bell pepper, finely chopped
- 1 large white onion, finely chopped
- 2 tbsp. pizza sauce
- Dried oregano and chilli flakes for seasoning
- Salt and pepper to taste

HHHHHHHHHHHHHHHHHHHHHHHHHHHHHHHHHHHHHHH

**Preparation:**

1. Preheat the oven to 350°F.

2.  Spread a pizza sauce over pizza base and sprinkle mozzarella over each half. Add veggies to the pizza in an even layer. Add salt and pepper.

3. Now, place the pizza over oven's grill.

4.  Bake for 15 minutes or until cheese melts down completely and turn golden brown.

5. Once ready, remove the pizza from oven.

6. Season with dried oregano and chilli flakes.

7.  Then, transfer the pizza to a serving platter and make 6 equal slices with the help of a pizza cutter

8. Serve hot!

# Recipe 6:  Pasta Pizza

Pizza topped with pasta in red sauce and cheese!

**Yield:** 6

**Prep Time:** 10 minutes

**Cook Time:** 15 minutes

**Ingredient List:**

- 1 medium pizza base
- 2 cups mozzarella cheese, grated
- 1 large green bell pepper, finely chopped
- 4 cup boiled macaroni pasta
- 1 cup pasta sauce
- 2 tbsp. pizza sauce
- Dried oregano and chilli flakes for seasoning
- Salt and pepper to taste

HHHHHHHHHHHHHHHHHHHHHHHHHHHHHHHHHHHHH

**Preparation:**

1.  Preheat the oven to 350°F.

2.  Combine pasta sauce and pasta in a bowl. Mix well and keep aside

3.  Spread a pizza sauce over pizza base and sprinkle mozzarella over each half. Add pasta to the pizza in an even layer. Add salt and pepper.

4.  Now, place the pizza over oven's grill.

5.  Bake for 15 minutes or until cheese melts down completely and turn golden brown.

6.  Once ready, remove the pizza from oven.

7.  Season with dried oregano and chilli flakes.

8.  Then, transfer the pizza to a serving platter and make 6 equal slices with the help of a pizza cutter

9.  Serve hot!

# Recipe 7:   French Bean and Tuna Pizza

Pizza with french beans and tuna flakes!

**Yield:** 6

**Prep Time:** 10 minutes

**Cook Time:** 15 minutes

**Ingredient List:**

- 1 medium pizza base
- 2 cups mozzarella cheese, grated
- 1 cup french beans, finely chopped

- 2 cups tuna flakes, finely chopped
- 2 tbsp. pizza sauce
- Dried oregano and chilli flakes for seasoning
- Salt and pepper to taste

HHHHHHHHHHHHHHHHHHHHHHHHHHHHHHHHHHHHHH

**Preparation:**

1.  Preheat the oven to 350°F.

2.  Spread a pizza sauce over pizza base and sprinkle mozzarella over each half. Add fresh beans and tuna to the pizza in an even layer. Add salt and pepper.

3.  Now, place the pizza over oven's grill.

4.  Bake for 15 minutes or until cheese melts down completely and turn golden brown.

5.  Once ready, remove the pizza from oven.

6.  Season with dried oregano and chilli flakes.

7.  Then, transfer the pizza to a serving platter and make 6 equal slices with the help of a pizza cutter

8.  Serve hot!

# Recipe 8:   Garlic Butter Pizza

Pizza topped with melted butter and chopped garlic!

**Yield:** 6

**Prep Time:** 10 minutes

**Cook Time:** 15 minutes

**Ingredient List:**

- 1 medium pizza base
- 2 cups mozzarella cheese, grated
- ½ cup melted butter
- 2 tbsp. garlic, finely chopped
- 2 tbsp. pizza sauce
- Dried oregano and chilli flakes for seasoning
- Salt and pepper to taste

HHHHHHHHHHHHHHHHHHHHHHHHHHHHHHHHHHHHH

**Preparation:**

1.  Preheat the oven to 350°F.

2.  Spread a pizza sauce over pizza base and sprinkle mozzarella over each half. Add butter and garlic to the pizza in an even layer. Add salt and pepper.

3.  Now, place the pizza over oven's grill.

4.  Bake for 15 minutes or until cheese melts down completely and turn golden brown.

5.  Once ready, remove the pizza from oven.

6.  Season with dried oregano and chilli flakes.

7.  Then, transfer the pizza to a serving platter and make 6 equal slices with the help of a pizza cutter

8.  Serve hot!

# Recipe 9:  Spring Onion and Cheddar Pizza

Pizza with spring onions and cheddar cheese!

**Yield:** 6

**Prep Time:** 10 minutes

**Cook Time:** 15 minutes

**Ingredient List:**

- 1 medium pizza base
- 2 cups mozzarella cheese, grated
- 2-3 spring onions, finely chopped
- 2 cups cheddar cheese, grated
- 2 tbsp. pizza sauce
- Dried oregano and chilli flakes for seasoning

- Salt and pepper to taste

HHHHHHHHHHHHHHHHHHHHHHHHHHHHHHHHHHHHHH

**Preparation:**

1. Preheat the oven to 350ºF.

2. Spread a pizza sauce over pizza base and sprinkle mozzarella over each half. Add onion and cheddar cheese to the pizza in an even layer. Add salt and pepper.

3. Now, place the pizza over oven's grill.

4. Bake for 15 minutes or until cheese melts down completely and turn golden brown.

5. Once ready, remove the pizza from oven.

6. Season with dried oregano and chilli flakes.

7. Then, transfer the pizza to a serving platter and make 6 equal slices with the help of a pizza cutter

8. Serve hot!

# Recipe 10:  Mango Pizza

Pizza topped with mango and cream cheese mix!

**Yield:** 6

**Prep Time:** 10 minutes

**Cook Time:** 15 minutes

**Ingredient List:**

- 1 medium pizza base
- 1 cup cream cheese
- 2 cups mango finely chopped

ННННННННННННННННННННННННННННННННННННН

**Preparation:**

1. Preheat the oven to 350°F.

2.  Combine mango and cream cheese in a bowl.

3.  Spread the prepared mix over pizza base.

4.  Now, place the pizza over oven's grill.

5.  Bake for 10 minutes.

6.  Once ready, remove the pizza from oven.

7.  Then, transfer the pizza to a serving platter and make 6 equal slices with the help of a pizza cutter.

8.  Serve hot!

# Recipe 11:   Cheese Pizza

Goat cheese, parmesan and mozzarella cheese pizza!

**Yield:** 6

**Prep Time:** 10 minutes

**Cook Time:** 15 minutes

**Ingredient List:**

- 1 medium pizza base
- 2 cups mozzarella cheese, grated
- 1 cup goat cheese
- 1 cup parmesan cheese

- 2 tbsp. pizza sauce
- Dried oregano and chilli flakes for seasoning
- Salt and pepper to taste

HHHHHHHHHHHHHHHHHHHHHHHHHHHHHHHHHHHHHH

**Preparation:**

1. Preheat the oven to 350°F.

2. Spread a pizza sauce over pizza base and sprinkle mozzarella over each half. Add goat cheese and parmesan cheese to the pizza in an even layer. Add salt and pepper.

3. Now, place the pizza over oven's grill.

4. Bake for 15 minutes or until cheese melts down completely and turn golden brown.

5. Once ready, remove the pizza from oven.

6. Season with dried oregano and chilli flakes.

7. Then, transfer the pizza to a serving platter and make 6 equal slices with the help of a pizza cutter

8. Serve hot!

# Recipe 12:  Pizza Sandwich

Boiled chickpea and white onion toppings pizza!

**Yield:** 6

**Prep Time:** 10 minutes

**Cook Time:** 15 minutes

**Ingredient List:**

- 2 medium pizza base
- 4 cups mozzarella cheese, grated
- 1 cup white onion, finely chopped
- 1 cup green bell pepper, finely chopped
- 1 cup lettuce, finely chopped

- 2 cups cooked meat of your choice
- 2 tbsp. pizza sauce
- Dried oregano and chilli flakes for seasoning
- Salt and pepper to taste

HHHHHHHHHHHHHHHHHHHHHHHHHHHHHHHHHHHHH

**Preparation:**

1. Preheat the oven to 350°F.

2. Spread a pizza sauce over pizza base and sprinkle 2 cups of mozzarella over each half. Add meat and veggies to the pizza in an even layer. Add salt and pepper.

3. Then, add rest of the cheese and place the other base of pizza on the top. Bast the pizza top with butter.

4. Now, place the pizza over oven's grill.

5. Bake for 15 minutes or until cheese melts down completely and the top turns golden brown.

6. Once ready, remove the pizza from oven.

7. Season with dried oregano and chilli flakes.

8. Then, transfer the pizza to a serving platter and make 6 equal slices with the help of a pizza cutter.

9. Serve hot!

# Recipe 13:  Aubergine Pizza

Grilled aubergine and white onion pizza!

**Yield:** 6

**Prep Time:** 10 minutes

**Cook Time:** 15 minutes

**Ingredient List:**

- 1 medium pizza base
- 2 cups mozzarella cheese, grated
- 2 cups finely chopped aubergine, grilled
- 1 large white onion, finely chopped
- 2 tbsp. pizza sauce
- Dried oregano and chilli flakes for seasoning
- Salt and pepper to taste

HHHHHHHHHHHHHHHHHHHHHHHHHHHHHHHHHHHHHHHH

**Preparation:**

1. Preheat the oven to 350ºF.

2.  Spread a pizza sauce over pizza base and sprinkle mozzarella over each half. Add veggies to the pizza in an even layer. Add salt and pepper.

3. Now, place the pizza over oven's grill.

4.  Bake for 15 minutes or until cheese melts down completely and turn golden brown.

5. Once ready, remove the pizza from oven.

6. Season with dried oregano and chilli flakes.

7.  Then, transfer the pizza to a serving platter and make 6 equal slices with the help of a pizza cutter

8. Serve hot!

# Recipe 14: Barbecue Chicken Pizza

Chicken in barbecue sauce pizza!

**Yield:** 6

**Prep Time:** 10 minutes

**Cook Time:** 15 minutes

**Ingredient List:**

- 1 medium pizza base
- 2 cups mozzarella cheese, grated
- ½ pound roasted chicken, shredded

- ½ cup barbecue sauce
- 2 tbsp. pizza sauce
- Dried oregano and chilli flakes for seasoning
- Salt and pepper to taste

HHHHHHHHHHHHHHHHHHHHHHHHHHHHHHHHHHHHHH

**Preparation:**

1. Preheat the oven to 350°F.

2. Combine chicken and barbecue sauce in a bowl. Mix well and keep aside

3. Spread a pizza sauce over pizza base and sprinkle mozzarella over each half. Add chicken to the pizza in an even layer. Add salt and pepper.

4. Now, place the pizza over oven's grill.

5. Bake for 15 minutes or until cheese melts down completely and turn golden brown.

6. Once ready, remove the pizza from oven.

7. Season with dried oregano and chilli flakes.

8. Then, transfer the pizza to a serving platter and make 6 equal slices with the help of a pizza cutter.

9. Serve hot!

# Recipe 15:   Egg Pizza

Pizza with chopped hardboiled eggs and pizza sauce!

**Yield:** 6

**Prep Time:** 10 minutes

**Cook Time:** 15 minutes

**Ingredient List:**

- 1 medium pizza base
- 2 cups mozzarella cheese, grated
- 4 hardboiled eggs, peeled and chopped
- 2 tbsp. pizza sauce
- Dried oregano and chilli flakes for seasoning
- Salt and pepper to taste

## Preparation:

1.  Preheat the oven to 350°F.

2.  Spread a pizza sauce over pizza base and sprinkle mozzarella over each half. Add hardboiled eggs to the pizza in an even layer. Add salt and pepper.

3.  Now, place the pizza over oven's grill.

4.  Bake for 15 minutes or until cheese melts down completely and turn golden brown.

5.  Once ready, remove the pizza from oven.

6.  Season with dried oregano and chilli flakes.

7.  Then, transfer the pizza to a serving platter and make 6 equal slices with the help of a pizza cutter

8.  Serve hot!

# Recipe 16:   Pepperoni Pizza

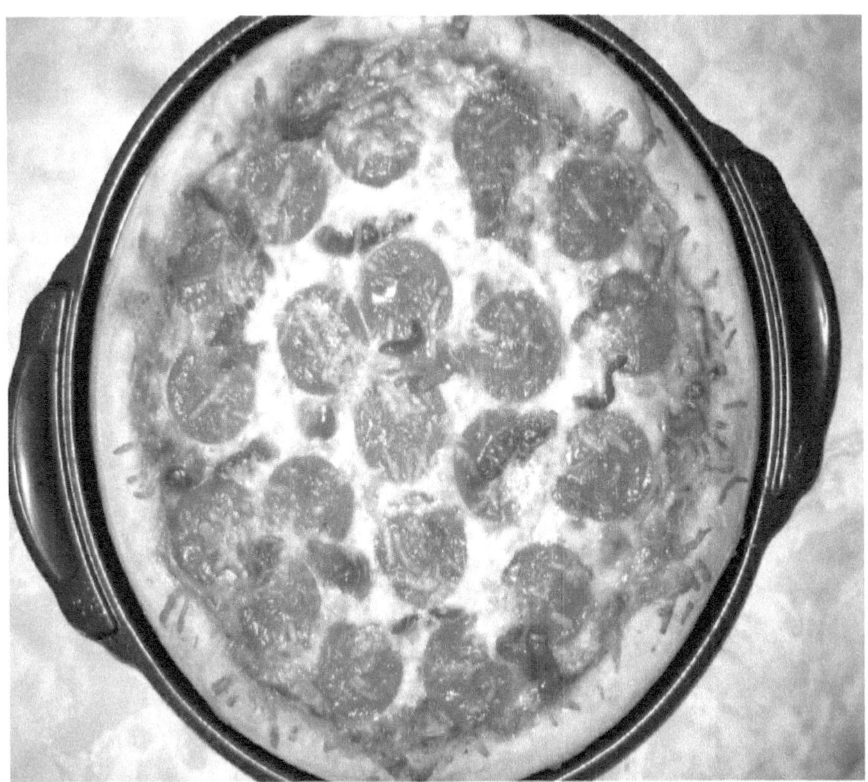

Pizza with mozzarella cheese and pepperoni slices!

**Yield:** 6

**Prep Time:** 10 minutes

**Cook Time:** 15 minutes

**Ingredient List:**

- 1 medium pizza base
- 2 cups mozzarella cheese, grated
- 18-20 pepperoni slices
- 2 tbsp. pizza sauce
- Dried oregano and chilli flakes for seasoning
- Salt and pepper to taste

## Preparation:

1. Preheat the oven to 350°F.

2. Spread a pizza sauce over pizza base and sprinkle mozzarella over each half. Add pepperoni to the pizza in an even layer. Add salt and pepper.

3. Now, place the pizza over oven's grill.

4. Bake for 15 minutes or until cheese melts down completely and turn golden brown.

5. Once ready, remove the pizza from oven.

6. Season with dried oregano and chilli flakes.

7. Then, transfer the pizza to a serving platter and make 6 equal slices with the help of a pizza cutter

8. Serve hot!

# Recipe 17:  French Fries Pizza

Pizza topped with french fries!

**Yield:** 6

**Prep Time:** 10 minutes

**Cook Time:** 15 minutes

**Ingredient List:**

- 1 medium pizza base
- 2 cups mozzarella cheese, grated
- ¼ pound french fried
- 2 tbsp. pizza sauce
- Dried oregano and chilli flakes for seasoning
- Salt and pepper to taste

HHHHHHHHHHHHHHHHHHHHHHHHHHHHHHHHHHHH

**Preparation:**

1.  Preheat the oven to 350°F.

2.  Spread a pizza sauce over pizza base and sprinkle mozzarella over each half. Add french fries to the pizza in an even layer. Add salt and pepper.

3.  Now, place the pizza over oven's grill.

4.  Bake for 15 minutes or until cheese melts down completely and turn golden brown.

5.  Once ready, remove the pizza from oven.

6.  Season with dried oregano and chilli flakes.

7.  Then, transfer the pizza to a serving platter and make 6 equal slices with the help of a pizza cutter

8.  Serve hot!

# Recipe 18:   Blue Cheese and Chorizo Pizza

Pizza with blue cheese and chorizo!

**Yield:** 6

**Prep Time:** 10 minutes

**Cook Time:** 15 minutes

**Ingredient List:**

- 1 medium pizza base
- 2 cups mozzarella cheese, grated
- 1 cup blue cheese, grated
- 1 cup chorizo, crumbled
- 2 tbsp. pizza sauce
- Dried oregano and chilli flakes for seasoning
- Salt and pepper to taste

## Preparation:

1. Preheat the oven to 350°F.

2. Spread a pizza sauce over pizza base and sprinkle mozzarella over each half. Add blue cheese and chorizo to the pizza in an even layer. Add salt and pepper.

3. Now, place the pizza over oven's grill.

4. Bake for 15 minutes or until cheese melts down completely and turn golden brown.

5. Once ready, remove the pizza from oven.

6. Season with dried oregano and chilli flakes.

7. Then, transfer the pizza to a serving platter and make 6 equal slices with the help of a pizza cutter

8. Serve hot!

# Recipe 19: Nachos Pizza

Pizza topped with corn nachos and extra cheese!

**Yield:** 6

**Prep Time:** 10 minutes

**Cook Time:** 15 minutes

**Ingredient List:**

- 1 medium pizza base
- 4 cups mozzarella cheese, grated
- ¼ pound corn nachos
- 2 tbsp. pizza sauce
- Dried oregano and chilli flakes for seasoning
- Salt and pepper to taste

## Preparation:

1. Preheat the oven to 350°F.

2. Spread a pizza sauce over pizza base and sprinkle 2 cups of mozzarella over each half. Add nachos to the pizza in an even layer.

3. Then, add remaining cheese to the pizza. Add salt and pepper.

4. Now, place the pizza over oven's grill.

5. Bake for 15 minutes or until cheese melts down completely and turn golden brown.

6. Once ready, remove the pizza from oven.

7. Season with dried oregano and chilli flakes.

8. Then, transfer the pizza to a serving platter and make 6 equal slices with the help of a pizza cutter.

9. Serve hot!

# Recipe 20: Minced Beef and Black Olive Pizza

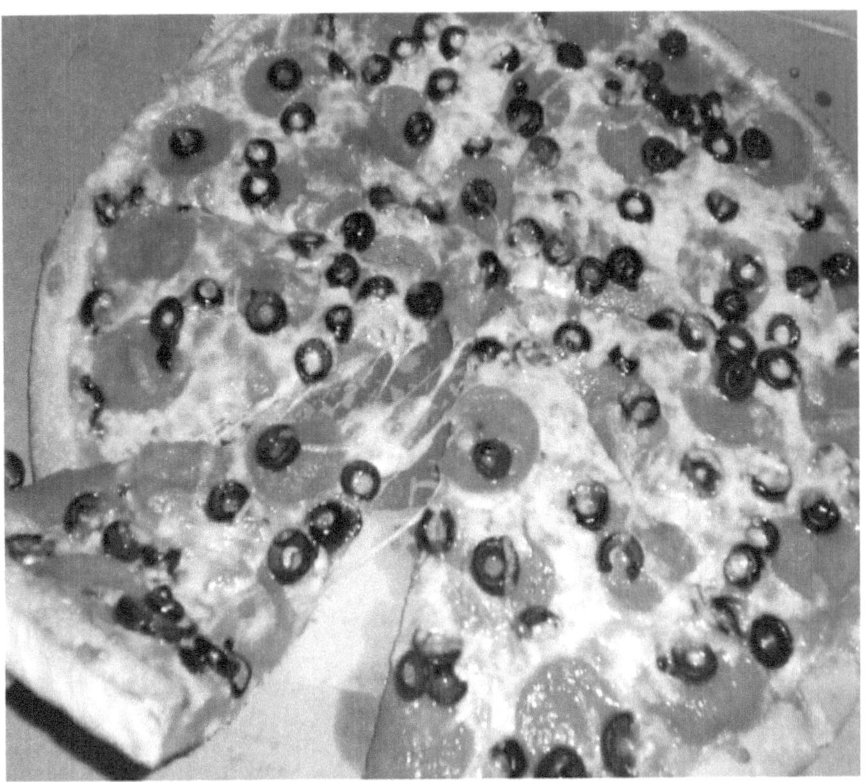

Stir fried minced beef and black olive pizza!

**Yield:** 6

**Prep Time:** 10 minutes

**Cook Time:** 15 minutes

**Ingredient List:**

- 1 medium pizza base
- 2 cups mozzarella cheese, grated
- 2 cups stir fried minced beef
- 1 cup black olives, chopped
- 2 tbsp. pizza sauce

- Dried oregano and chilli flakes for seasoning
- Salt and pepper to taste

HHHHHHHHHHHHHHHHHHHHHHHHHHHHHHHHHHHH

**Preparation:**

1. Preheat the oven to 350ºF.

2. Spread a pizza sauce over pizza base and sprinkle mozzarella over each half. Add beef and olives to the pizza in an even layer. Add salt and pepper.

3. Now, place the pizza over oven's grill.

4. Bake for 15 minutes or until cheese melts down completely and turn golden brown.

5. Once ready, remove the pizza from oven.

6. Season with dried oregano and chilli flakes.

7. Then, transfer the pizza to a serving platter and make 6 equal slices with the help of a pizza cutter

8. Serve hot!

# Recipe 21:   Bean Pizza

Pizza topped with baked beans in red sauce!

**Yield:** 6

**Prep Time:** 10 minutes

**Cook Time:** 15 minutes

**Ingredient List:**

- 1 medium pizza base
- 2 cups mozzarella cheese, grated
- 2 cups baked beans in tomato sauce
- 2 tbsp. pizza sauce
- Dried oregano and chilli flakes for seasoning
- Salt and pepper to taste

HHHHHHHHHHHHHHHHHHHHHHHHHHBeHHHHHHHHHHHHHH

**Preparation:**

1.  Preheat the oven to 350°F.

2.  Spread a pizza sauce over pizza base and sprinkle mozzarella over each half. Add baked beans to the pizza in an even layer. Add salt and pepper.

3.  Now, place the pizza over oven's grill.

4.  Bake for 15 minutes or until cheese melts down completely and turn golden brown.

5.  Once ready, remove the pizza from oven.

6.  Season with dried oregano and chilli flakes.

7.  Then, transfer the pizza to a serving platter and make 6 equal slices with the help of a pizza cutter

8.  Serve hot!

# Recipe 22:   3 Pepper Pizza

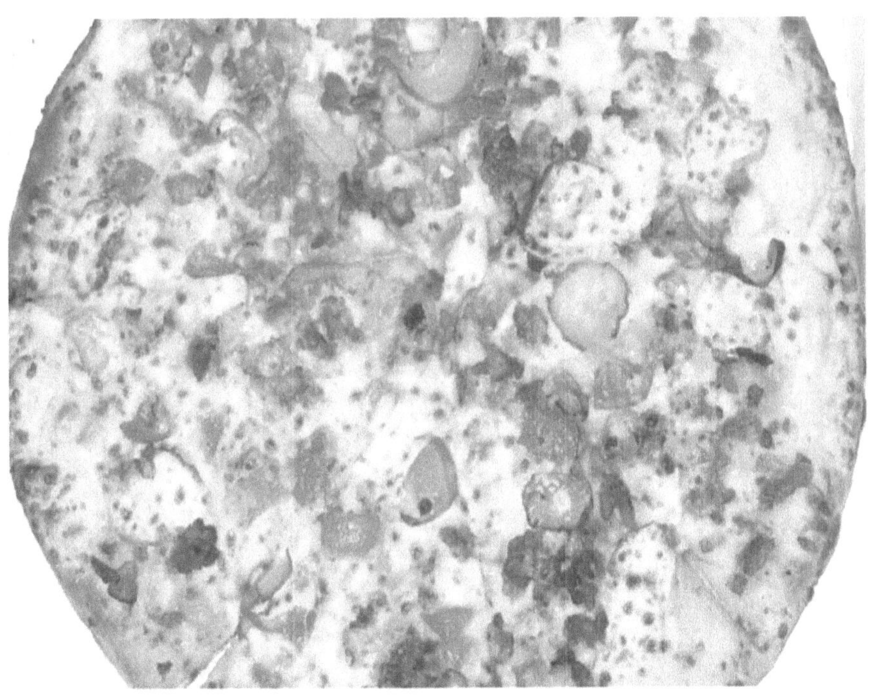

Jalapeños, cayenne and yellow bell pepper pizza!

**Yield:** 6

**Prep Time:** 10 minutes

**Cook Time:** 15 minutes

**Ingredient List:**

- 1 medium pizza base
- 2 cups mozzarella cheese, grated
- 1 cup jalapeno peppers, sliced
- 1 cup cayenne peppers, sliced
- 1 cup yellow bell pepper
- 2 tbsp. pizza sauce
- Dried oregano and chilli flakes for seasoning
- Salt and pepper to taste

HHHHHHHHHHHHHHHHHHHHHHHHHHHHHHHHHHHHHHH

**Preparation:**

1.  Preheat the oven to 350°F.

2.  Spread a pizza sauce over pizza base and sprinkle mozzarella over each half. Add peppers to the pizza in an even layer. Add salt and pepper.

3.  Now, place the pizza over oven's grill.

4.  Bake for 15 minutes or until cheese melts down completely and turn golden brown.

5.  Once ready, remove the pizza from oven.

6.  Season with dried oregano and chilli flakes.

7.  Then, transfer the pizza to a serving platter and make 6 equal slices with the help of a pizza cutter

8.  Serve hot!

# Recipe 23:   Dry Fruit Pizza

Pizza topped with assorted dry fruits and sour cream mix!

**Yield:** 6

**Prep Time:** 10 minutes

**Cook Time:** 15 minutes

**Ingredient List:**

- 1 medium pizza base
- ½ cup raisins
- ½ cup cashews, roughly chopped
- ½ cup almond, roughly chopped
- 1 cup sour cream

HHHHHHHHHHHHHHHHHHHHHHHHHHHHHHHHHHHHHH

**Preparation:**

1. Preheat the oven to 350°F.

2. Combine all the ingredients in a bowl except pizza.

3. Spread the prepared mix over pizza base.

4. Now, place the pizza over oven's grill.

5. Bake for 10 minutes.

6. Once ready, remove the pizza from oven.

7. Then, transfer the pizza to a serving platter and make 6 equal slices with the help of a pizza cutter.

8. Serve hot!

# Recipe 24:   Pork and Jalapeños Pizza

Stir fried pork and jalapeños pizza!

**Yield:** 6

**Prep Time:** 10 minutes

**Cook Time:** 15 minutes

**Ingredient List:**

- 1 medium pizza base
- 2 cups mozzarella cheese, grated
- ½ pound stir fried pork
- 1 cup jalapeno, sliced
- 2 tbsp. pizza sauce
- Dried oregano and chilli flakes for seasoning
- Salt and pepper to taste

**Preparation:**

1. Preheat the oven to 350°F.

2. Spread a pizza sauce over pizza base and sprinkle mozzarella over each half. Add pork and jalapeños to the pizza in an even layer. Add salt and pepper.

3. Now, place the pizza over oven's grill.

4. Bake for 15 minutes or until cheese melts down completely and turn golden brown.

5. Once ready, remove the pizza from oven.

6. Season with dried oregano and chilli flakes.

7. Then, transfer the pizza to a serving platter and make 6 equal slices with the help of a pizza cutter

8. Serve hot!

# Recipe 25:  Squash Pizza

Pizza topped with squash spaghetti in white sauce!

**Yield:** 6

**Prep Time:** 10 minutes

**Cook Time:** 15 minutes

**Ingredient List:**

- 1 medium pizza base
- 2 cups mozzarella cheese, grated
- ¼ pound boiled squash spaghetti
- 1 cup white pasta sauce
- 2 tbsp. pizza sauce
- Dried oregano and chilli flakes for seasoning
- Salt and pepper to taste

ͰͰͰͰͰͰͰͰͰͰͰͰͰͰͰͰͰͰͰͰͰͰͰͰͰͰͰͰͰͰͰͰͰͰͰͰͰͰ

**Preparation:**

1. Preheat the oven to 350°F.

2. Combine spaghetti and white pasta sauce in a bowl. Mix well and keep aside.

3. Spread a pizza sauce over pizza base and sprinkle mozzarella over each half. Add spaghetti to the pizza in an even layer. Add salt and pepper.

4. Now, place the pizza over oven's grill.

5. Bake for 15 minutes or until cheese melts down completely and turn golden brown.

6. Once ready, remove the pizza from oven.

7. Season with dried oregano and chilli flakes.

8. Then, transfer the pizza to a serving platter and make 6 equal slices with the help of a pizza cutter

9. Serve hot!

# Recipe 26:   Chocolate Pizza

Pizza topped with cocoa powder, castor sugar and milk mix!

**Yield:** 6

**Prep Time:** 10 minutes

**Cook Time:** 15 minutes

**Ingredient List:**

- 1 medium pizza base
- ½ cup cocoa powder
- 1 cup castor sugar

- 1 cup milk

HHHHHHHHHHHHHHHHHHHHHHHHHHHHHHHHHHHHH

**Preparation:**

1. Preheat the oven to 350ºF.

2. Combine cocoa, castor sugar and milk in a bowl. Mix well and keep aside

3. Spread a prepared mix over pizza base in an even layer.

4. Now, place the pizza over oven's grill.

5. Bake for 10 minutes.

6. Once ready, remove the pizza from oven.

7. Then, transfer the pizza to a serving platter and make 6 equal slices with the help of a pizza cutter.

8. Serve hot!

# Recipe 27: Pumpkin Pizza

Pizza topped with pumpkin and roasted pumpkin seeds!

**Yield:** 6

**Prep Time:** 10 minutes

**Cook Time:** 15 minutes

**Ingredient List:**

- 1 medium pizza base
- 2 cups mozzarella cheese, grated
- 2 cups pumpkin, finely chopped
- 1 cup roasted pumpkin seeds
- 2 tbsp. pizza sauce
- Dried oregano and chilli flakes for seasoning

- Salt and pepper to taste

HHHHHHHHHHHHHHHHHHHHHHHHHHHHHHHHHHHHHHH

## Preparation:

1.  Preheat the oven to 350°F.

2.  Spread a pizza sauce over pizza base and sprinkle mozzarella over each half. Add pumpkin and seeds to the pizza in an even layer. Add salt and pepper.

3.  Now, place the pizza over oven's grill.

4.  Bake for 15 minutes or until cheese melts down completely and turn golden brown.

5.  Once ready, remove the pizza from oven.

6.  Season with dried oregano and chilli flakes.

7.  Then, transfer the pizza to a serving platter and make 6 equal slices with the help of a pizza cutter

8.  Serve hot!

# Recipe 28:   Double Cheese Margarita Pizza

Pizza topped with mozzarella cheese and pizza sauce!

**Yield:** 6

**Prep Time:** 10 minutes

**Cook Time:** 15 minutes

**Ingredient List:**

- 1 medium pizza base
- 4cups mozzarella cheese, grated
- 4 tbsp. pizza sauce
- Dried oregano and chilli flakes for seasoning
- Salt and pepper to taste

HHHHHHHHHHHHHHHHHHHHHHHHHHHHHHHHHHHHH

**Preparation:**

1.  Preheat the oven to 350°F.

2. Spread a 2-tbsp. pizza sauce over pizza base and sprinkle half of the mozzarella over each half. Add remaining pizza sauce and then, add remaining cheese to the pizza in an even layer. Add salt and pepper.

3. Now, place the pizza over oven's grill.

4. Bake for 15 minutes or until cheese melts down completely and turn golden brown.

5. Once ready, remove the pizza from oven.

6. Season with dried oregano and chilli flakes.

7. Then, transfer the pizza to a serving platter and make 6 equal slices with the help of a pizza cutter

8. Serve hot!

# Recipe 29:  Mint and Coriander Pizza

Pizza topped with fresh coriander and mint leaves!

**Yield:** 6

**Prep Time:** 10 minutes

**Cook Time:** 15 minutes

**Ingredient List:**

- 1 medium pizza base
- 2 cups mozzarella cheese, grated
- 1 cup fresh mint leaves, finely chopped
- 2 cups fresh coriander leaves, finely chopped
- 2 tbsp. pizza sauce
- Dried oregano and chilli flakes for seasoning
- Salt and pepper to taste

HHHHHHHHHHHHHHHHHHHHHHHHHHHHHHHHHHHHHH

**Preparation:**

1. Preheat the oven to 350°F.

2. Spread a pizza sauce over pizza base and sprinkle mozzarella over each half. Add mint and coriander leaves to the pizza in an even layer. Add salt and pepper.

3. Now, place the pizza over oven's grill.

4. Bake for 15 minutes or until cheese melts down completely and turn golden brown.

5. Once ready, remove the pizza from oven.

6. Season with dried oregano and chilli flakes.

7. Then, transfer the pizza to a serving platter and make 6 equal slices with the help of a pizza cutter

8. Serve hot!

# Recipe 30: Salmon and Corn Pizza

Stir fried salmon chunks and corn kernels pizza!

**Yield:** 6

**Prep Time:** 10 minutes

**Cook Time:** 15 minutes

**Ingredient List:**

- 1 medium pizza base
- 2 cups mozzarella cheese, grated
- 2 cups stir fried salmon chunks
- 1 cup corn kernels
- 2 tbsp. pizza sauce
- Dried oregano and chilli flakes for seasoning
- Salt and pepper to taste

HHHHHHHHHHHHHHHHHHHHHHHHHHHHHHHHHHHHHH

**Preparation:**

1.  Preheat the oven to 350ºF.

2.  Spread a pizza sauce over pizza base and sprinkle mozzarella over each half. Add salmon and corn kernels to the pizza in an even layer. Add salt and pepper.

3.  Bake for 15 minutes or until cheese melts down completely and turn golden brown.

4.  Once ready, remove the pizza from oven.

5.  Season with dried oregano and chilli flakes.

6.  Then, transfer the pizza to a serving platter and make 6 equal slices with the help of a pizza cutter

7.  Serve hot!

# Recipe 31:   Ham and Sage Pizza

Pizza topped with ham and sage!

**Yield:** 6

**Prep Time:** 10 minutes

**Cook Time:** 15 minutes

**Ingredient List:**

- 1 medium pizza base
- 2 cups mozzarella cheese, grated
- 2 cups ham, finely chopped
- Handful of fresh sage leaves, finely chopped
- 2 tbsp. pizza sauce
- Dried oregano and chilli flakes for seasoning
- Salt and pepper to taste

HHHHHHHHHHHHHHHHHHHHHHHHHHHHHHHHHHHHH

**Preparation:**

1.  Preheat the oven to 350°F.

2.  Spread a pizza sauce over pizza base and sprinkle mozzarella over each half. Add ham and sage to the pizza in an even layer. Add salt and pepper.

3.  Now, place the pizza over oven's grill.

4.  Bake for 15 minutes or until cheese melts down completely and turn golden brown.

5.  Once ready, remove the pizza from oven.

6.  Season with dried oregano and chilli flakes.

7.  Then, transfer the pizza to a serving platter and make 6 equal slices with the help of a pizza cutter

8.  Serve hot!

# Recipe 32:   Fruit Pizza

Pizza topped with pineapple, strawberries and apple!

**Yield:** 6

**Prep Time:** 10 minutes

**Cook Time:** 15 minutes

**Ingredient List:**

- 1 medium pizza base
- ½ cup strawberries, hulled and finely chopped
- ½ cup pineapple, finely chopped
- ½ cup apple, finely chopped
- 1 cup sour cream

HHHHHHHHHHHHHHHHHHHHHHHHHHHHHHHHHHHHHHH

**Preparation:**

1.  Preheat the oven to 350ºF.

2.  Combine all the ingredients in a bowl except pizza.

3.  Spread the prepared mix over pizza base.

4.  Now, place the pizza over oven's grill.

5.  Bake for 10 minutes.

6.  Once ready, remove the pizza from oven.

7.  Then, transfer the pizza to a serving platter and make 6 equal slices with the help of a pizza cutter.

8.  Serve hot!

# Recipe 33:   Parsley Pizza

Pizza topped with green leafy parsley leaves!

**Yield:** 6

**Prep Time:** 10 minutes

**Cook Time:** 15 minutes

**Ingredient List:**

- 1 medium pizza base
- 2 cups mozzarella cheese, grated
- 2 cups fresh parsley leaves, finely chopped
- 2 tbsp. pizza sauce
- Dried oregano and chilli flakes for seasoning
- Salt and pepper to taste

HHHHHHHHHHHHHHHHHHHHHHHHHHHHHHHHHHHHH

**Preparation:**

1.  Preheat the oven to 350°F.

2.  Spread a pizza sauce over pizza base and sprinkle mozzarella over each half. Add parsley to the pizza in an even layer. Add salt and pepper.

3.  Now, place the pizza over oven's grill.

4.  Bake for 15 minutes or until cheese melts down completely and turn golden brown.

5.  Once ready, remove the pizza from oven.

6.  Season with dried oregano and chilli flakes.

7.  Then, transfer the pizza to a serving platter and make 6 equal slices with the help of a pizza cutter

8.  Serve hot!

# Recipe 34:   Cauliflower and Green Pea Pizza

Grated cauliflower and boiled green pea pizza!

**Yield:** 6

**Prep Time:** 10 minutes

**Cook Time:** 15 minutes

**Ingredient List:**

- 1 medium pizza base
- 2 cups mozzarella cheese, grated
- 1 small head of cauliflower, grated
- 1 cup boiled green peas
- 2 tbsp. pizza sauce
- Dried oregano and chilli flakes for seasoning
- Salt and pepper to taste

HHHHHHHHHHHHHHHHHHHHHHHHHHHHHHHHHHHHHH

**Preparation:**

1. Preheat the oven to 350°F.

2. Spread a pizza sauce over pizza base and sprinkle mozzarella over each

half. Add veggies to the pizza in an even layer. Add salt and pepper.

3.  Now, place the pizza over oven's grill.

4.  Bake for 15 minutes or until cheese melts down completely and turn golden brown.

5.  Once ready, remove the pizza from oven.

6.  Season with dried oregano and chilli flakes.

7.  Then, transfer the pizza to a serving platter and make 6 equal slices with the help of a pizza cutter

8.  Serve hot!

# Recipe 35:   Ricotta Cheese and Lemon Grass Pizza

Crumbled ricotta cheese and finely chopped fresh lemon grass pizza!

**Yield:** 6

**Prep Time:** 10 minutes

**Cook Time:** 15 minutes

**Ingredient List:**

- 1 medium pizza base
- 2 cups mozzarella cheese, grated
- 2 cups ricotta cheese, crumbled
- 2 tbsp. freshly chopped lemon grass
- 2 tbsp. pizza sauce
- Dried oregano and chilli flakes for seasoning
- Salt and pepper to taste

HHHHHHHHHHHHHHHHHHHHHHHHHHHHHHHHHHHHHH

**Preparation:**

1.  Preheat the oven to 350ºF.

2.  Spread a pizza sauce over pizza base and sprinkle mozzarella over each half. Add ricotta cheese and lemon grass to the pizza in an even layer. Add salt and pepper.

3.  Now, place the pizza over oven's grill.

4.  Bake for 15 minutes or until cheese melts down completely and turn golden brown.

5.  Once ready, remove the pizza from oven.

6.  Season with dried oregano and chilli flakes.

7.  Then, transfer the pizza to a serving platter and make 6 equal slices with the help of a pizza cutter

8.  Serve hot!

# Recipe 36: Chicken and Pineapple Pizza

Roasted chicken and pineapple pizza!

**Yield:** 6

**Prep Time:** 10 minutes

**Cook Time:** 15 minutes

**Ingredient List:**

- 1 medium pizza base
- 2 cups mozzarella cheese, grated
- ½ pound roasted chicken, shredded
- 1 cup pineapple, finely chopped
- 2 tbsp. pizza sauce
- Dried oregano and chilli flakes for seasoning
- Salt and pepper to taste

HHHHHHHHHHHHHHHHHHHHHHHHHHHHHHHHHHHHHH

**Preparation:**

1.  Preheat the oven to 350°F.

2.  Spread a pizza sauce over pizza base and sprinkle mozzarella over each half. Add chicken and pineapple to the pizza in an even layer. Add salt and pepper.

3.  Now, place the pizza over oven's grill.

4.  Bake for 15 minutes or until cheese melts down completely and turn golden brown.

5.  Once ready, remove the pizza from oven.

6.  Season with dried oregano and chilli flakes.

7.  Then, transfer the pizza to a serving platter and make 6 equal slices with the help of a pizza cutter

8.  Serve hot!

# Recipe 37: Salami Pizza

Chopped chicken salami and cheese pizza!

**Yield:** 6

**Prep Time:** 10 minutes

**Cook Time:** 15 minutes

**Ingredient List:**

- 1 medium pizza base
- 2 cups mozzarella cheese, grated
- ¼ pound chicken salami, chopped
- 2 tbsp. pizza sauce
- Dried oregano and chilli flakes for seasoning
- Salt and pepper to taste

## Preparation:

1. Preheat the oven to 350°F.

2. Spread a pizza sauce over pizza base and sprinkle mozzarella over each half. Add chopped salami to the pizza in an even layer. Add salt and pepper.

3. Now, place the pizza over oven's grill.

4. Bake for 15 minutes or until cheese melts down completely and turn golden brown.

5. Once ready, remove the pizza from oven.

6. Season with dried oregano and chilli flakes.

7. Then, transfer the pizza to a serving platter and make 6 equal slices with the help of a pizza cutter

8. Serve hot!

# Recipe 38:   Pork Sausage Pizza

Chopped pork sausage and onion pizza!

**Yield:** 6

**Prep Time:** 10 minutes

**Cook Time:** 15 minutes

**Ingredient List:**

- 1 medium pizza base
- 2 cups mozzarella cheese, grated
- 2 cups pork sausage, chopped
- 1 large white onion, finely chopped
- 2 tbsp. pizza sauce
- Dried oregano and chilli flakes for seasoning
- Salt and pepper to taste

НННННННННННННННННННННННННННННННННННННННН

**Preparation:**

1. Preheat the oven to 350°F.

2. Spread a pizza sauce over pizza base and sprinkle mozzarella over each half. Add pork sausage and white onion to the pizza in an even layer. Add salt and pepper.

3. Now, place the pizza over oven's grill.

4. Bake for 15 minutes or until cheese melts down completely and turn golden brown.

5. Once ready, remove the pizza from oven.

6. Season with dried oregano and chilli flakes.

7. Then, transfer the pizza to a serving platter and make 6 equal slices with the help of a pizza cutter

8. Serve hot!

# Recipe 39:   Turkey and Carrot Pizza

Pizza topped with roasted turkey and grated carrots!

**Yield:** 6

**Prep Time:** 10 minutes

**Cook Time:** 15 minutes

**Ingredient List:**

- 1 medium pizza base
- 2 cups mozzarella cheese, grated
- 2 cups roasted turkey, shredded
- 2 cups carrot, grated
- 2 tbsp. pizza sauce
- Dried oregano and chilli flakes for seasoning
- Salt and pepper to taste

HHHHHHHHHHHHHHHHHHHHHHHHHHHHHHHHHHHHHH

**Preparation:**

1.  Preheat the oven to 350ºF.

2.  Spread a pizza sauce over pizza base and sprinkle mozzarella over each half. Add turkey and carrots to the pizza in an even layer. Add salt and pepper.

3.  Now, place the pizza over oven's grill.

4.  Bake for 15 minutes or until cheese melts down completely and turn golden brown.

5.  Once ready, remove the pizza from oven.

6.  Season with dried oregano and chilli flakes.

7.  Then, transfer the pizza to a serving platter and make 6 equal slices with the help of a pizza cutter

8.  Serve hot!

# Recipe 40:   White Button Mushroom and Black Olive Pizza

White button mushrooms and sliced black olive pizza!

**Yield:** 6

**Prep Time:** 10 minutes

**Cook Time:** 15 minutes

**Ingredient List:**

- 1 medium pizza base
- 2 cups mozzarella cheese, grated
- 2 cup white button mushrooms, chopped
- 1 cup black olives, sliced
- 2 tbsp. pizza sauce
- Dried oregano and chilli flakes for seasoning
- Salt and pepper to taste

НННННННННННННННННННННННННННННННННННННННННН

**Preparation:**

1.  Preheat the oven to 350°F.

2.  Spread a pizza sauce over pizza base and sprinkle mozzarella over each half. Add veggies to the pizza in an even layer. Add salt and pepper.

3.  Now, place the pizza over oven's grill.

4.  Bake for 15 minutes or until cheese melts down completely and turn golden brown.

5.  Once ready, remove the pizza from oven.

6.  Season with dried oregano and chilli flakes.

7.  Then, transfer the pizza to a serving platter and make 6 equal slices with the help of a pizza cutter

8.  Serve hot!

# Recipe 41:  Goat Pizza

Fried goat chucks and mozzarella cheese pizza!

**Yield:** 6

**Prep Time:** 10 minutes

**Cook Time:** 15 minutes

**Ingredient List:**

- 1 medium pizza base
- 2 cups mozzarella cheese, grated
- 2 cups stir fried goat chunks
- 2 tbsp. pizza sauce
- Dried oregano and chilli flakes for seasoning
- Salt and pepper to taste

HHHHHHHHHHHHHHHHHHHHHHHHHHHHHHHHHHHHHHHH

**Preparation:**

1. Preheat the oven to 350ºF.

2. Spread a pizza sauce over pizza base and sprinkle mozzarella over each half. Add goats chunks to the pizza in an even layer. Add salt and pepper.

3. Now, place the pizza over oven's grill.

4. Bake for 15 minutes or until cheese melts down completely and turn golden brown.

5. Once ready, remove the pizza from oven.

6. Season with dried oregano and chilli flakes.

7. Then, transfer the pizza to a serving platter and make 6 equal slices with the help of a pizza cutter

8. Serve hot!

# Recipe 42: Roasted Duck Pizza

Roasted duck pizza with mozzarella cheese and pizza sauce!

**Yield:** 6

**Prep Time:** 10 minutes

**Cook Time:** 15 minutes

**Ingredient List:**

- 1 medium pizza base
- 2 cups mozzarella cheese, grated
- 1 roasted duck, shredded
- 2 tbsp. pizza sauce
- Dried oregano and chilli flakes for seasoning
- Salt and pepper to taste

## Preparation:

1.  Preheat the oven to 350°F.

2.  Spread a pizza sauce over pizza base and sprinkle mozzarella over each half. Add roasted duck to the pizza in an even layer. Add salt and pepper.

3.  Now, place the pizza over oven's grill.

4.  Bake for 15 minutes or until cheese melts down completely and turn golden brown.

5.  Once ready, remove the pizza from oven.

6.  Season with dried oregano and chilli flakes.

7.  Then, transfer the pizza to a serving platter and make 6 equal slices with the help of a pizza cutter

8.  Serve hot!

# Recipe 43:  Zucchini Pizza

Pizza topped with zucchini and mozzarella!

**Yield:** 6

**Prep Time:** 10 minutes

**Cook Time:** 15 minutes

**Ingredient List:**

- 1 medium pizza base
- 2 cups mozzarella cheese, grated
- ½ pound zucchini, finely chopped
- 2 tbsp. pizza sauce
- Dried oregano and chilli flakes for seasoning
- Salt and pepper to taste

## Preparation:

1. Preheat the oven to 350°F.

2. Spread a pizza sauce over pizza base and sprinkle mozzarella over each half. Add zucchini to the pizza in an even layer. Add salt and pepper.

3. Now, place the pizza over oven's grill.

4. Bake for 15 minutes or until cheese melts down completely and turn golden brown.

5. Once ready, remove the pizza from oven.

6. Season with dried oregano and chilli flakes.

7. Then, transfer the pizza to a serving platter and make 6 equal slices with the help of a pizza cutter

8. Serve hot!

# Recipe 44:   Falafel Pizza

Pizza topped with falafel balls and cheese!

**Yield:** 6

**Prep Time:** 10 minutes

**Cook Time:** 15 minutes

**Ingredient List:**

- 1 medium pizza base
- 2 cups mozzarella cheese, grated
- 15-20 falafel balls (1x1 inch)
- 2 tbsp. pizza sauce
- Dried oregano and chilli flakes for seasoning
- Salt and pepper to taste

## Preparation:

1.  Preheat the oven to 350ºF.

2.  Spread a pizza sauce over pizza base and sprinkle mozzarella over each half. Add falafels to the pizza in an even layer. Add salt and pepper.

3.  Now, place the pizza over oven's grill.

4.  Bake for 15 minutes or until cheese melts down completely and turn golden brown.

5.  Once ready, remove the pizza from oven.

6.  Season with dried oregano and chilli flakes.

7.  Then, transfer the pizza to a serving platter and make 6 equal slices with the help of a pizza cutter

8.  Serve hot!

# Recipe 45:   Baby Corn and Prawn Pizza

Pizza topped with butter fried prawns and baby corns!

**Yield:** 6

**Prep Time:** 10 minutes

**Cook Time:** 15 minutes

**Ingredient List:**

- 1 medium pizza base
- 2 cups mozzarella cheese, grated
- ¼ pound butter fried prawns
- ¼ pound baby corns, chopped
- 2 tbsp. pizza sauce
- Dried oregano and chilli flakes for seasoning
- Salt and pepper to taste

HHHHHHHHHHHHHHHHHHHHHHHHHHHHHHHHHHHHHHH

## Preparation:

1.  Preheat the oven to 350°F.

2.  Spread a pizza sauce over pizza base and sprinkle mozzarella over each half. Add prawns and baby corns to the pizza in an even layer. Add salt and pepper.

3.  Now, place the pizza over oven's grill.

4.  Bake for 15 minutes or until cheese melts down completely and turn golden brown.

5.  Once ready, remove the pizza from oven.

6.  Season with dried oregano and chilli flakes.

7.  Then, transfer the pizza to a serving platter and make 6 equal slices with the help of a pizza cutter

8.  Serve hot!

# Recipe 46:  Asparagus and Potato Pizza

Boiled asparagus and potato pizza!

**Yield:** 6

**Prep Time:** 10 minutes

**Cook Time:** 15 minutes

**Ingredient List:**

- 1 medium pizza base
- 2 cups mozzarella cheese, grated
- 2 cups boiled asparagus, finely chopped
- 1 medium boiled potato, peeled and finely chopped
- 2 tbsp. pizza sauce
- Dried oregano and chilli flakes for seasoning
- Salt and pepper to taste

## Preparation:

1. Preheat the oven to 350°F.

2. Spread a pizza sauce over pizza base and sprinkle mozzarella over each half. Add veggies to the pizza in an even layer. Add salt and pepper.

3. Now, place the pizza over oven's grill.

4. Bake for 15 minutes or until cheese melts down completely and turn golden brown.

5. Once ready, remove the pizza from oven.

6. Season with dried oregano and chilli flakes.

7. Then, transfer the pizza to a serving platter and make 6 equal slices with the help of a pizza cutter

8. Serve hot!

# Recipe 47:  Spinach and Tomato Pizza

Pizza topped with baby spinach leaves and cherry tomatoes!

**Yield:** 6

**Prep Time:** 10 minutes

**Cook Time:** 15 minutes

**Ingredient List:**

- 1 medium pizza base
- 2 cups mozzarella cheese, grated
- ¼ pound baby spinach leaves, finely chopped
- 2 cup cherry tomatoes, halved
- 2 tbsp. pizza sauce
- Dried oregano and chilli flakes for seasoning
- Salt and pepper to taste

HHHHHHHHHHHHHHHHHHHHHHHHHHHHHHHHHHHHHH

**Preparation:**

1.  Preheat the oven to 350ºF.

2.  Spread a pizza sauce over pizza base and sprinkle mozzarella over each half. Add veggies to the pizza in an even layer. Add salt and pepper.

3.  Now, place the pizza over oven's grill.

4.  Bake for 15 minutes or until cheese melts down completely and turn golden brown.

5.  Once ready, remove the pizza from oven.

6.  Season with dried oregano and chilli flakes.

7.  Then, transfer the pizza to a serving platter and make 6 equal slices with the help of a pizza cutter

8.  Serve hot!

# Recipe 48: Lentil Pizza

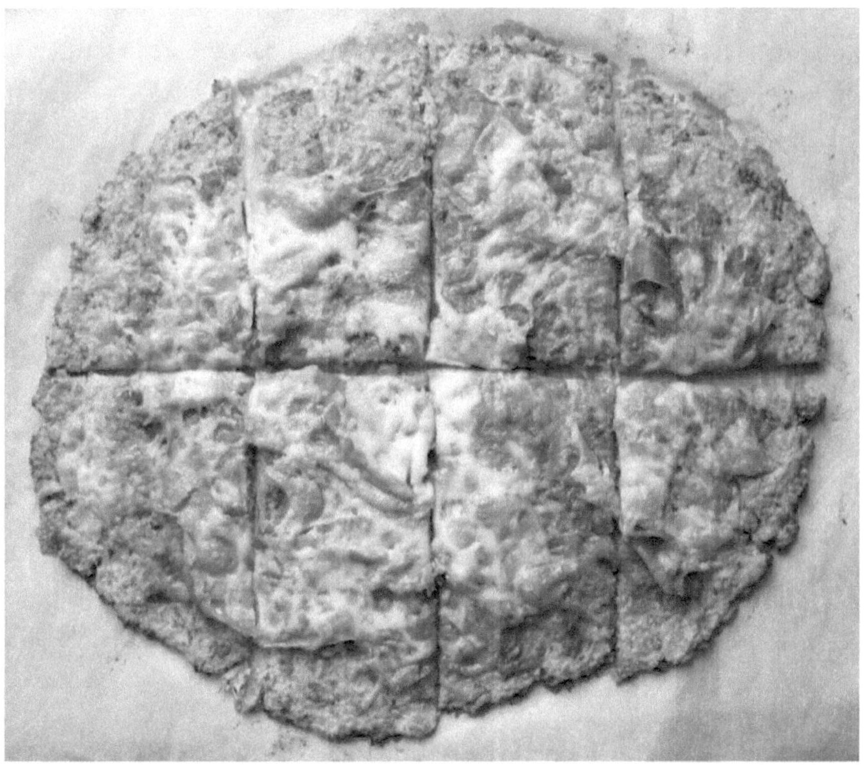

Boiled lentils and cheese pizza!

**Yield:** 6

**Prep Time:** 10 minutes

**Cook Time:** 15 minutes

**Ingredient List:**

- 1 medium pizza base
- 2 cups mozzarella cheese, grated
- 2 cup boiled lentils
- 2 tbsp. pizza sauce
- Dried oregano and chilli flakes for seasoning
- Salt and pepper to taste

НННННННННННННННННННННННННННННННННННННННН

**Preparation:**

1.  Preheat the oven to 350ºF.

2.  Spread a pizza sauce over pizza base and sprinkle mozzarella over each half. Add lentils to the pizza in an even layer. Add salt and pepper.

3.  Now, place the pizza over oven's grill.

4.  Bake for 15 minutes or until cheese melts down completely and turn golden brown.

5.  Once ready, remove the pizza from oven.

6.  Season with dried oregano and chilli flakes.

7.  Then, transfer the pizza to a serving platter and make 6 equal slices with the help of a pizza cutter

8.  Serve hot!

# Recipe 49: Stir Fried Tuna Pizza

**Yield:** 6

**Prep Time:** 10 minutes

**Cook Time:** 15 minutes

**Ingredient List:**

- 1 medium pizza base
- 2 cups mozzarella cheese, grated
- 1 large green bell pepper, finely chopped
- 1 large white onion, finely chopped
- 2 tbsp. pizza sauce
- Dried oregano and chilli flakes for seasoning

- Salt and pepper to taste

HHHHHHHHHHHHHHHHHHHHHHHHHHHHHHHHHHHHHH

**Preparation:**

1.  Preheat the oven to 350°F.

2.  Spread a pizza sauce over pizza base and sprinkle mozzarella over each half. Add veggies to the pizza in an even layer. Add salt and pepper.

3.  Now, place the pizza over oven's grill.

4.  Bake for 15 minutes or until cheese melts down completely and turn golden brown.

5.  Once ready, remove the pizza from oven.

6.  Season with dried oregano and chilli flakes.

7.  Then, transfer the pizza to a serving platter and make 6 equal slices with the help of a pizza cutter

8.  Serve hot!

# Recipe 50:  Cherry Tomato and Basil Pizza

Pizza topped with curry tomatoes and basil leaves!

**Yield:** 6

**Prep Time:** 10 minutes

**Cook Time:** 15 minutes

**Ingredient List:**

- 1 medium pizza base
- 2 cups mozzarella cheese, grated
- 2 cup cherry tomatoes, halved
- 1 cup fresh basil leaves
- 2 tbsp. pizza sauce
- Dried oregano and chilli flakes for seasoning
- Salt and pepper to taste

## Preparation:

1. Preheat the oven to 350ºF.

2. Spread a pizza sauce over pizza base and sprinkle mozzarella over each half. Add tomatoes and basil leaves to the pizza in an even layer. Add salt and pepper.

3. Now, place the pizza over oven's grill.

4. Bake for 15 minutes or until cheese melts down completely and turn golden brown.

5. Once ready, remove the pizza from oven.

6. Season with dried oregano and chilli flakes.

7. Then, transfer the pizza to a serving platter and make 6 equal slices with the help of a pizza cutter

8. Serve hot!